Breaking the Chains

A Tool to Promote and Enhance Healthy Relationships Between Adults and Children

By: Robert L. Daniels

Contents

I dedicate this book to my wife and kids who I love dearly. Also to my Grandmother and Aunt BJ who are looking down on me from heaven.

Foreword

I have known Robert Daniels for quite a while. He is my husband, best friend, and the father of our children. Robert has always been so special. This is a person who loves people, leads with compassion, showcases kindness, and is always trying to better himself. Robert is a father of four (all boys), and I watch him strive every single day to make a difference in our kids' lives. He is super passionate about really tapping into listening to them, figuring out what they are passionate about, watering their gifts, and really trying to create and build the connection between parent and child. I am so proud to witness this firsthand. Robert had a very rough upbringing, which is one of the reasons why he is so passionate about Breaking the Chains of dysfunction and bridging the gap between adults and kids.

When Robert first came to me about the book idea, I couldn't help but think who better to write about Breaking the Chains and creating better adult and kid relationships. This is something that he does and is more than qualified and capable of speaking on this subject. I also couldn't help but think how beneficial a book like this would be to so many people, including myself. There are so many parents who really struggle to connect with their children or children that they may work with. For example, when our house is a mess and things in the house are out of order, I literally blow my top. I will probably start yelling telling the kids, Robert, and everyone to get the house together, no questions asked. Robert, on the other hand, will walk to the kids and ask them what's up. He will ask them what happened to the house, why does it look like this. So instead of jumping to conclusions, he talks to them first. Most of the time, when he does this, there is actually a good reason for the mess. He takes this approach all the time, and this little approach believe it or not, helps you connect with your children.

Beyond writing this foreword, my involvement in this book consisted of me going through the exercises and practicing them daily. I really made them a part of my daily life, and honestly, it works. Sometimes as adults, we don't think that the kids deserve respect also. We often have the mentality of what I say goes, but thinking like that does not break the chains nor build the bond. I have learned this and so much more through my husband and this book.

I am beyond excited about this book and what it can do. I know this firsthand as it has significantly helped me. I am so proud of my husband Robert Daniels for staying dedicated and determined to write this book. I am always so amazed at how passionate he is and about how much I have learned from him. I hope you enjoy it and learn from it as much as I did. Thank you, babe, for allowing me to be part of this amazing project that will change lives and Break Chains.

Breaking the Chains

Introduction

"I was raised like that, and I turned out just fine." How often have you heard someone say something like this? More importantly, what are they really saying when these words come out of their mouths? Before you answer that, I want to be clear about my intentions. I wrote this book for parents looking for a better way to raise their children than their parents raised them — essentially breaking the chains of dysfunction and abuse.

Who am I to speak on such a topic? Here's some background: my grandmother raised me. Heroin killed my mother and my father too. Addiction and dysfunction have twisted and even destroyed relationships in my family. I survived a life filled with trauma, abuse, and feelings of failure and worthlessness.

Now, many years later, I'm walking into my stride. I have four sons, a lovely wife, and a beautiful home filled with love. I believe there are some key things that helped me overcome where others would have failed. In other words... I've been through some stuff. No, I'm not a Harvard professor or a therapist. I'm just a guy who had to figure out how to survive in a world of chaos. Based on my experiences, it's safe to say that I have a pretty good inclination of what this change *should* look like.

This book is geared toward parents raising adolescents and teenagers in single or two-parent households. Although that's the primary focus, this book can also go for anyone who finds themselves in a mentoring position. Yes, that means teachers, counselors, and even coaches can benefit from what I have to share with you. I want this book to be a survival guide for making your relationship with your kids a lasting, loving piece of your life.

I am definitely not perfect. I previously had the mentality that if my children have clothes on their back, food to eat and a roof over their heads, that's enough and I am a great parent because of that. It wasn't until my oldest son came to me one day and told me that I am a great provider, but that I had never tried to tap into his mind and try to really understand him. That was an eye-opening moment for me. I instantly got to work on correcting everything that I felt I was doing wrong and really tapping into my children to the next level.

Through trial and error, I developed a system that can be used by any adult who wants to enhance the communication with the children in their lives. A system that, if implemented correctly, will make everyone sleep better, love harder, and worry less. With this in mind, *Breaking the Chains* was formed. Now, I invite you to take a look at how you can incorporate these same things into your life.

As a quick recap, this book is for :

- Students
- Faculty
- Parents
- Mentors
- Older siblings
- Grandparents
- Godparents
- Aunts and Uncles

I believe there is a middle ground, and I believe we can reach it together. It's not just the child, the mentor, or the parent. We are all struggling to reach each other. This struggle is a lot like a chain. It ultimately holds us back from what we're wanting to accomplish. In this book, we are going to *break* the chains. We are going to build bridges that help us communicate better than ever. Most importantly, we are going to break generational curses that have plagued our community for years. We're finally going to break the chains of what *has* been to make way for what *should* be—a better environment for our kids to grow and achieve greatness.

Good luck! I pray that by the time you finish this book, you will be filled with ideas that motivate and empower YOU.

Chapter 1
Defining What's Important

I am a husband and a father of four sons. As you can imagine, my attention was turned entirely towards being a provider. Yes, it is important. I must provide, but there is additional work that comes along with that when you have children.

Once upon a time, all I did was work, work, work. I hustled between two and three jobs just to provide.

I'm fortunate today to have been afforded more time so that this is no longer my reality. Now I spend more time with my family, and I'm working to understand them better. I realized that when I wasn't spending time with my kids, I also wasn't challenging them to grow into their gifts.

Gift Inventory

There are two types of gifts. The first are natural-born gifts. Natural born gifts just mean talent, like what you tend to see with many singers. The second are gifts born from interest and diligent practice. These gifts only become apparent after time is spent practicing and burnishing a skillset to the point it becomes expertise. Let me give you a personal example to help you understand a little more.

My natural-born gift was my ability to sing. In fact, music runs in my family. By the time I was two years old, I was humming with one of my aunties while she was on the piano. My grandmother was a gospel singer, and she watered my natural abilities by having me join our church's choir.

She kept me singing, and then my auntie would work with me from time to time by letting me hear notes on the piano to see if I could match it with my voice. I also went to many of my aunt and uncles' concert performances, and I'd watched and learned from them.

It really wasn't until I got to the ninth grade that I discovered my gift with athletics. It was my school's track coach who noticed it. When Coach first saw me run, I was chasing after a schoolmate who stole from me. Coach would later recall saying at the time, "That boy is fast. I want to bring him out to the track and see what he can do."

Prior to that moment, I knew nothing about track and field. I tried out for the team, made it, and I became fascinated with track and field ever since. Coach was very hardcore; he was an athlete who specialized in track and field—hurdles in particular. His passion for the sport and the fact he took an interest in me was what captured my attention.

From there, Coach encouraged me to tap into this new-found gift for running so that I could excel at almost any sport. Basically, an adult saw something promising in me, praised me for it, then showed me how to put the gift to use. Praise and encouragement are mandatory to a child's self-esteem. Combine that with discipline; we get excellence.

My family encouraged my natural gift in music, and my coach encouraged my abilities in track and field. These are healthy examples of how to push a child forward, especially when they are utilizing their gifts. We have to push and inspire our children. That push can mean the difference between a successful child and a child that does not accomplish much in life.

"Every child has something they do well." - RD

Each of my sons has a unique gift. I believe these gifts will help them in life. As parents, we sometimes overlook our children's gifts. We overlook these gifts because their gift may be unique, or it may be something that we do every day as an average person. When you know your child's gifts, you can help them improve those gifts.

Always remember to keep this in mind:

- Some children are organizers
- Some kids are game players
- Some children are athletes
- Some children have musical talent

It's important as a parent or mentor to understand *your* child's gifts and help them grow those gifts. This is important in your effort to help your child.

Exercise: Gift Inventory

For each of your children, list their gifts. Try to list at least three gifts per child.

1.

2.

3.

Now answer three important questions about their gifts

1. When and where do they use their gifts?

_____

_____

_____

_____

_____

_____

_____

_____

_____

_____

_____

_____

_____

_____

_____

_____

_____

_____

_____

2. On a day when they use one or more of their gifts, what do you notice about them?

- What is their personality like?

- Are they happy?

- Do they appear more confident?

_____

_____

_____

_____

_____

_____

_____

_____

_____

_____

_____

_____

_____

_____

_____

_____

_____

_____

3. Do you think they would use their gifts more often if they felt challenged or had an opportunity to compete?

_____

_____

_____

_____

_____

_____

_____

_____

_____

_____

_____

_____

_____

_____

_____

_____

_____

_____

_____

_____

_____

_____

4. Do they use their gifts to help other people?

_____

_____

_____

_____

_____

_____

_____

_____

_____

_____

_____

_____

_____

_____

_____

_____

_____

_____

_____

_____

_____

_____

_____

_____

The more positive interaction children have with their gifts, the more confidence they begin to build. Confidence leads us to the topic of the next chapter, PUSH.

SUMMARY - GIFTS

- It's important as a parent that you understand your child's gifts

- Gifts can be natural or learned from repetition

- In this chapter, we showed you how to:

    1) Identify their gifts and unique talents.

    2) Pull back and look at how they use their gifts.

    3) Observe how your child's gifts make them feel.

Chapter 2
Push to the Limit

This chapter is called "PUSH" because I believe that this is something important we have to do with our kids. We have to push and inspire them if we want them to reach new levels. That push can make the difference between a successful child and a child that does not accomplish much in life. Now, allow me to address what it means to push your kid.

Many of our kids feel like no one cares about their feelings. Some of this comes from our lack of time and attention. When a child feels that no one cares about those exciting gifts listed in Chapter 1, then the excitement begins to fade. In fact, your child may become *more* distracted. I've watched my sons at different times become distracted with things that are both positive and negative—and far away from their gifts.

Keeping children busy in the areas of their talents and gifts is also important to their emotional intelligence. A child's emotional intelligence is the ability to emotionally understand that people care, they matter to others, their decisions have an impact, and most importantly, they are responsible for everything they do.

By pushing children, we begin to show them that they can take a simple gift and turn it into something that makes them more successful in different areas of their life.

We also begin to show them that we care about their progress and success. I think it is important for children to see that someone cares because it makes them feel challenged to take their lives and what they're doing to new levels.

Positive Push Practices

Practice #1: Schedule Time

How do you push your children in a positive way? You push them by making time for what is important to them and scheduling time to enjoy that activity.

Practice #2: Talk

Talk to your children and encourage them daily. Even if you only have five minutes a day together, use that time to listen and talk to them. Be careful when your kids tell you about something important to them that you don't immediately criticize their thoughts. Criticism leads to reduced cooperation in the long run, which is something you don't want.

While talking to kids about something important, don't role switch. Role switching is when you alternate between being a disciplinarian and a listening parent. When you do this, they lose trust in you. They grow fearful that talking to you will get them in trouble. Stay in the listening parent mode and just let them share.

Believe it or not, most kids want you to challenge and encourage them.

Why do they need a positive PUSH?

Some people think that PUSH means the parent begins to care and aggressively gets involved with the child. I believe PUSH is about helping kids see their role. No matter what you're discussing with your kid, if they don't feel they have a responsibility, then they won't do their best work. My goal has always been to help my kids deliver their best work.

"The only way to bring out the best is to push me." My oldest son actually said this to me. Before we reached that point, though, we had all types of issues. He had trouble with his behavior, poor grades, constantly seeming distracted, and challenging communication.

I did three things to help my oldest son shift:

- The first was to listen to him uninterrupted and

undistracted. Listening opens doors that parents can enter.

- The second thing I did was that I took what I heard from him, and I found a way to incorporate it into his daily activities that helped him.

- The third and final thing was I held him accountable for the results. I made *his* life *his* responsibility.

This process was tough because teenage boys think they are invincible. If you find yourself with stubborn children like this, don't give up. Instead, be assertive with what your expectations are and what they should expect from themselves. I made it clear that his failures were not a direct correlation to our relationship. Instead, his failures would be based on him not asking the right questions.

As much as we want to, it's almost impossible to help someone who doesn't ask for it. Therefore, instill that trait in your children as quickly as you can. Another thing I told him was his failures would be based on his effort. Simply put: no effort, no results.

Positive Push and Discipline

I come from a background filled with abuse. More specifically, beatings were used as a disciplinary tactic. A tactic to gain compliance or obedience is ridiculous to me. I don't agree with it. I'm not down with it. There's nothing that can change my mind about that. It teaches violence, and it breaks a child. You can beat a child into submission, but you can't beat a child to success. If you want to see your child succeed, invest in them—that's positive pushing.

Here's an example. Our oldest son RJ is an avid online gamer who belongs to a gaming team. They engage in matches with other teams. They have gotten so good that they've established a reputation. RJ approached us about turning their gaming success into a branding success. He asked us, "How do I get a trademark?" He said that he and his teammates want to become an actual business and have their own business account. Our way of pushing them was to help them form their own Limited Liability Company.

At the time, we would occasionally find random transactions on our bank statements because he was using our bank card and Paypal for gaming activities. After setting up the LLC, we opened a bank account for him to help him make and keep track of his transactions more efficiently. Guess what? It worked like a charm.

Hold your children accountable for results. Make *their* life *their* responsibility.

Responsibility means taking ownership of the things that are in your care. As parents, if we want our children to take responsibility for living their best life, we start by giving them small responsibilities that gradually become bigger as they grow older. The ideal result is that they will prove themselves able to shoulder such responsibilities, then we hold them accountable to it. I learned growing up that everybody in a household has their particular responsibilities, including children. Whether it's in a household, at school, or on a sports team, everyone has a role to play. Furthermore, no matter which role you personally have, you're responsible for it.

I think for me, growing up the way that I did, I have to be responsible for myself. I had to wake up every day to brush my teeth and wash my face. I understood that I had to be at school at a certain time. These are just a handful of responsibilities I carried as a child. Although times have changed, the roles haven't. You have to regularly remind your children of their responsibilities. Like when you wake up one minute and come back an hour later to find they're still not up. You're mad at them, but you also need to hold them accountable.

Sometimes I think parents are afraid to give their kids responsibility. They know they could do the task better or faster themselves, so they decide to just help the kids out. Stop! Let them take ownership and understand that their handling of responsibility is not just a reflection of them but also a reflection of the entire family.

Exercise 2.1: PUSH Your Child

1. What things do you notice about your child that are indicators that they may not understand their responsibility? List the indicators for each child.

_____

_____

_____

_____

_____

_____

_____

_____

_____

_____

_____

_____

_____

_____

_____

_____

_____

_____

_____

_____

_____

2. How has your child's lack of responsibility affected the family?

_____

_____

_____

_____

_____

_____

_____

_____

_____

_____

_____

_____

_____

_____

_____

_____

_____

_____

_____

_____

_____

_____

3. Describe your child's roles and responsibilities to the family.

_____

_____

_____

_____

_____

_____

_____

_____

_____

_____

_____

_____

_____

_____

_____

_____

_____

_____

_____

_____

_____

_____

SUMMARY – PUSH TO THE LIMIT

- Pushing and encouraging makes children feel good

- Pushing builds a child's emotional intelligence

- Pushing keeps children focused on the things they do well

- Pushing eliminates distractions

- Pushing helps to hold children accountable while establishing trust

Chapter 3
Core Values

Core values didn't play a huge role when I was younger because I did not understand their true meaning. Core values are principles by which you abide and are expectations by which you never waiver. Core values were very far from my mind until I was around the age of 21. I started a new job, and I realized that they had a particular set of traits and ideas by which everyone abided. Every day I saw people throughout the company using the company's core values as a blueprint for success. In my head, I asked myself, *Why don't I have some core values for my life?*

Of course, I had no real reason why I shouldn't, so I got to work. I created a set of core values based on the things that were the nearest and dear to me, and I believe they have really helped me make better decisions over the years. I'm better, and my family is better by adhering to these values.

Core values help you take an introspective look at yourself. They keep you organized and in alignment with your "why." If core values can help companies reach higher levels of success, they can surely help families in other ways. In our family, the core values we hold paramount include respect for authority, integrity, discipline, and generosity. These are the primary character traits we aimed to shape in our children to ensure their safety and success. I know having a set of core values can help you and your children as well. Take a look below at some of our core values explained in detail.

Respect for Authority

Traditionally, the way parents taught children respect and obedience, if not deference to authority, was by literally beating it into them. Respect for authority is one of the earliest lessons a child learns. It was very literal because parents at one time would beat their child over an unsatisfactory display of respect or deference to them. These were lessons learned through beatings.

Integrity

Like most children, my son reached a point where fitting in was very important. He made a decision to do something that compromised his integrity. Little did he know, what is done in the dark will always come to light. He took money out of my wallet without asking. He handed me my coat, and when I went to my wallet, the money wasn't there. I knew there could only have been one person who could have taken it. I didn't even second-guess it. Rather than confronting him immediately, I waited until the next morning before he left for school to confront him. The conversation went something like this:

"Hey. Did you take my money?" I asked him.

"No."

"Do you have any money on you? Let me check you."

He shifted his eyes and said, "Yeah, I have a little money."

"Where did you get it from?" I asked

"It was something, okay."

"Do you want to talk to me about this?"

He ended up breaking down and telling me the truth right then and there.

Instead of getting upset about it, we just talked about it and told him why he couldn't do that. He understood.

I wanted him to stop and realize that he could have gone to jail if this happened under different circumstances.

He thought I wouldn't notice the missing money. He needed to learn that the *consequences* of such miscalculations could be death. After our talk, he was confined to his room with no TV for a week. Remember, we must always hold them accountable for their actions and teach integrity.

Discipline

As a parent, you must evaluate what you're feeling, what you're dealing with, and know if your children are in a position to change. You also must determine what level of discipline is necessary. Not all kids need a harsh disciplinarian. The important thing is that you engage in conversation with them to grow their understanding of integrity as it relates to your own core values. This is a way of providing them guidance, building a relationship, and leading them to make better decisions on their own.

Generosity/Compassion

My grandmother raised me, and my grandmother had compassion for everybody she came in contact with— no matter who they were. I've seen some of her practices and lived by that example. It starts at home for us. I've never wanted to talk to my kids when I'm upset or when I'm so angry at them that I can't find the compassion within. I put myself in their shoes and try to understand the circumstances that shaped other people's choices.

I was a kid who was raised with less. Being an adolescent and seeing how my grandmother always gave to people no matter her circumstances truly impacted who I am today. You have to know there is always someone else who is worse off than you. Generosity is something that is instilled into our family and part of our DNA.

Exercise 3.1: Core Values

This exercise is intended to help you define your core values. If you have a set of core values you currently follow, this will give you a space to write and discuss them. If you have never identified core values for yourself, this will be a great exercise to help you do so. When you're done, you will have a better idea of what your values are and how they motivate you.

Step 1:

Write down up to 10 words that describe things you believe are important to your success. Below is an example.

1. Trustworthiness	Showing every day that I am genuinely someone that can be trusted.

Fill in the space below with your descriptive words

Word	Description of Its Impact on You as a Core Value
1	
2	
3	
4	
5	
6	
7	
8	
9	
10	

Step 2:

Use the list from Step 1 and identify your top 4 core values. List them here.

#	Word	Description
1		
2		
3		
4		

Step 3:

Discuss the values you identified with your family and close friends.

SUMMARY — CORE VALUES

- Core values help you take an introspective look at yourself

- Core values help to keep you organized and in alignment with what is important to you

- If core values can help companies reach higher levels of success, then surely they can help us

Chapter 4
Breaking the Chains

"Repeating the patterns of the past is a recipe for failure. Our goal is to help our children be more successful. We must break the chains of failure." RD

Parenting Code of Excellence Requirements

In 1977, my parents received the great news that I was about to come into this world. That news was short-lived because three months later, my father was murdered. This left my mom with big decisions to make about her life and my future. There was just one problem—she had a drug addiction that took over her life. She was unable to find clarity and freedom from her addiction. One month and eight days after I was born, my mother died from an overdose. Because of her drug use, I was born drug-addicted and left without parents. This was my first chain in life. It was the first barrier for me to overcome.

What I learned about life, I learned from relatives and from the streets. I knew that failure was not an option for me, so with the help of my grandmother, I learned to live by a code of excellence. This code changed my life. It gave me a chance to succeed. The code included five things that I used over and over to stay in the right lane in life.

Patience

You must trust that you can communicate and talk to your child. This requires intentional patience. Intentional patience is not yelling, having anxiety, or being short with your words when communicating with your child. Also, patience means not showing anger or feelings that would lead your child to believe you are upset with them. This affects how your child will respond in your conversations.

My code of excellence regarding patience was formed as part of a negative example my uncle made when I was a kid. In fact, each of my five codes of excellence was directly formed to combat a negative attribute I saw in my household growing up.

My uncle had no patience. He had no patience for anything. No patience for kids, just being kids. No patience for too much noise in the house. Essentially, his patience was completely nonexistent. Parents must have patience, and patience is acquired via humility and time.

Builder of Trust

In this section, you must understand that to help your child; they must trust the path you want them to follow. That means that trust will give you the ability to strengthen your child because your child believes in what you are sharing with them. Children will believe in what you share based on your daily habits and interactions with them. In the end, both of you will be stronger from making an effort to build trust in each other.

As a child, I was so scared. I was so fearful in my uncle's house. I didn't feel like I could talk to him about anything. All kinds of walls were instantly built because of the fear my uncle instilled in me. If he wanted to change his relationship with me, he could have done so by proving he wasn't going to hurt me. He could have shown that his goal was to be a listening ear with an open door policy. That would have built trust. If he were different, I would have been able to go to him and tell him what I was going through. I could have told him where my pain was, and he could have helped me figure it out.

Trust is like credit. Starting out, everyone starts out with *some* credit. That credit grows after establishing a history of making good decisions that include honoring commitments, acting with integrity, and acting responsibly. Your credit is damaged when you're caught lying, engaging in risky behaviors, and failing to honor commitments. Trust is earned, and it works both ways.

Have No Expectations

My children's lives are their lives. I'm here to guide them, give direction, and help them become independent. I'm not here to live their life, and you're not here to live your child's life either. This means that as parents as mentors, we have to give children room to make decisions. We must learn to give them this room because every decision comes with an experience. Every experience is a lesson. Having no expectations doesn't mean we don't want the best for our children. It just means they have a decision about the type of life they want to live. We are here to help them become independent, not live their life for them. They are in control, and we are just conductors trying to help guide the way.

Reserve Judgment

This one is challenging. I'm asking you to take a neutral position with your child. Before you stop reading, hear me out. If a child can't talk to you or share their feelings without being hit with a storm of criticism, they won't share anything with you. Conversations must start from a neutral zone, a safe and encouraging place. Our first instinct is to protect our children. This often causes us to take their words and use them as swords in a battle. I'm asking you instead to take their words and use them to heal their wounds. As hard as it may seem, you must reserve all judgment if you wish to keep the lines of communication open.

Work at Listening

Your children will be making decisions for the rest of their lives. Establishing yourself as a person, they can talk to is very important. When a child doesn't see you as someone to talk to, they exclude you from their decisions. Hence, you become a responder and not a team player.

Being a listener gives them a trusted loved one to pour out their feelings to, and it helps them make better decisions. Years from now, you want to be the person they come to when they make a decision, not the person they avoid.

In summary, my code of excellence comes from one of my biggest areas of pain as a child. I couldn't trust the adults around me. Most of this was the result of inconsistency in their behaviors. The five areas just discussed are things I believe are crucial to building a family bond. This bond is the root of growth and the foundation every family needs in order to break the chains of the past.

Fixing Your Family Starts with Better Communication

I am one of many parents who hated the way we were disciplined growing up. I believe success in parenting is separating from my past and using my own approach with my children. Communication is key to this goal, and I work at maintaining a good relationship with my boys.

My relationship with my uncle was defined by the fact that I did not respect his authority. Looking back, I realize this was due to his lack of communication. His way of disciplining me focused on punishment rather than growth. I felt the pain, but I rarely learned the lessons he was trying to impart. Over time, I became filled with resentment and anger. I completely blocked him out, and we didn't communicate at all except when I was in trouble.

If you only talk to your child when they are in trouble, they will only dread talking to you, believing that this latest talking-to moment is just a "gotcha" moment. I work toward decreasing my children's fear and raising their confidence. This is done by making every moment a time of healing and learning.

"When a child doesn't see you as someone to talk to, they exclude you from their decisions. Hence, you become a responder and not a team player." RD

Recognizing Emotional Walls

I learned early in life to protect myself by putting up emotional walls between my relatives and myself. I especially had a wall up to protect me from my uncle, not knowing that emotional walls disconnect families. The walls represented:

- Hurt
- Not feeling loved
- A comfortable zone

These three things were the recipe used to construct the brick walls I built up in life. The wall of hurt was simply a result of what was happening to me due to a lack of communication. This led to me ultimately not feeling loved. Our children need to know that they *are* loved. When they don't feel loved, their behavior reflects the lack of love.

For me, the lack of love led to seeking a comfort zone. My comfort zone was a place behind the emotional wall where I could hide. When I hid behind my wall, no one could see how I felt; no one could see my hurt. Many of our children hide behind a wall to protect themselves from the emotional pain they feel from relationships with their parents.

Here are the three actions I used to break down the walls with my boys.

Pay Attention

Pay attention to what you say to them and how you talk to them. That's big because a lot of parents think that all they have to do is curse the kid out to let them know "It's my way or the highway." That doesn't work with all kids. That is a form of abuse, and that is a form of parenting we have to break away from.

Praise

Praise them when they put their best foot forward and do the best job they could whether they had won or not. We must still congratulate them and tell them how proud we are of them. Make them feel like their voice matters—that *they* matter. Institute an open-door policy through which your kids can have access to you and tell you anything. Please remember, you are their guardian, their protector, and their first and primary mentor. As their guardian protector, your children must be able to find comfort in confiding in you about anything.

As a whole, we don't give our kids enough pats on the back. We don't tell them enough how proud we are of them. We neglect to express how happy we are that they got good grades or how happy we are that they won the race. As parents, mentors, and leaders, we have to give more praise to our children.

Make Their Voice Matter

As a child, it can be easy to feel like your voice doesn't matter when you talk with an adult who always talks over you or disregards your feelings. As parents, we must work to set aside the concept of parental authority. In short, this just means that what the parents say goes, and the child has no say in the matter. Doing this makes the child feel powerless and limits their will to be expressive. We do *not* want this for our children. We want them to feel like their opinions matter, even if you, as the parent, will have the final say.

Avoid relationship-destroying actions and behavior

Actions that can destroy relationships with your children include calling your children out of the name. Don't call your children the first thing that comes to your mind. Don't be overly critical of your child. Allow their mistakes to become teaching moments.

Let's say, for instance, you caught your child flashing gang signs on a video chat, smoking dope, or engaged in premarital sex. Going off on your child is the worst thing you could do. Take a deep breath. Take a moment to calm down before talking to your child. This is the moment you reiterate to your child that your role is to help them make better decisions.

The reality is that as long as your children are under your roof, you're responsible for them. As long as they are alive, you will love and protect them. Still, the only way you'll be able to protect your children is by avoiding scenarios that will cause your children to build up walls and ensuring free-flowing communication between you and them.

Exercise 4.1: Safe Circle

Create a safe circle of communication. This basically means setting aside a time during the week in which your family talks about what's going on in each of their respective lives. If your family is more than two people, set some additional time aside so that you can have one-on-one conversations with your children. Discuss the good things, the bad things, and the challenges. Be sure to be age-appropriate. Let this time be an open space for discussing the things that confuse them.

The goal of the exercise is to allow your children to communicate more effectively with you and allow yourself to respond to your children openly and honestly. Additionally, this is also a time when you can learn your child's communication habits intimately while speaking freely in a space lacking in tension.

HOW TO START YOUR SAFER SAFE CIRCLE CONVERSATIONS

Talk about how the week is going. We might start off with what someone did to offend us or what I didn't like about what happens with my day. It always starts with me because I'm the icebreaker. I could really just drop my load on them, which allows them to get an idea of what that should be like for them. They end up just responding and falling right in line by being very open. By open, my kids pretty much know my past, which is a lot to swallow. But they don't judge me for it. They don't make their own assumptions. They just understand their dad had a hard life, and he's trying to give us wisdom so we don't have to go through the same things that he went through.

When the parents speak, they should allow themselves to be vulnerable and open. They should talk about themselves and parts of their day and parts of their lives. This is also a way for the family's lore and the family's narrative to get passed on to the next generation. This is also a space where your child gets to see themselves in you.

Your challenge is to simply listen to your children and put yourself in their shoes. Listen to what they say with three things in mind: building trust, space, and respect. This will be discussed more in the next chapter as well.

EXPECTED RESULTS FOR PARENTS AND MENTORS

- Freedom to express yourself openly and honestly

- A better understanding of body language and communication habits of your child

- Less tension while talking to children

EXPECTED RESULTS FOR THE CHILD

- Trust in the parent and confidence that they will be able to communicate with the parent

- No judgment or criticism

How does this create a safe circle for your child?

Children need to feel safe. If a child feels safe, they will share more with you. Here is how you create that safe circle:

1. Let them know you are willing to listen.

2. Create a judgment-free environment.

3. Put yourself in their shoes and listen to their thoughts.

4. Break away from the "parent mode" or the authoritative mode. Listen at their level and give them a chance to open up.

This is why this exercise is so important. It will better connect you to your child by letting them lead the conversation and providing an environment that nurtures their thoughts.

Exercise 4.2: Identifying the Hurt

Write down the most hurtful things you heard from
your family growing up.

1. _____

_____

_____

_____

2. _____

_____

_____

_____

3. _____

_____

_____

_____

4. _____

_____

_____

_____

Now share in a few words how those statements made you feel?

1. _____
_____
_____
_____

2. _____
_____
_____
_____

3. _____
_____
_____
_____

4. _____
_____
_____
_____

Now take a moment and think about a few names you have called your child that hurt them.

1. _____

_____

_____

_____

2. _____

_____

_____

_____

3. _____

_____

_____

_____

4. _____

_____

_____

_____

How do you think hearing you call them that made them feel?

1. _____

_____

_____

_____

2. _____

_____

_____

_____

3. _____

_____

_____

_____

4. _____

_____

_____

_____

SUMMARY — BREAKING THE CHAINS

- You must set standards for yourself; I have a code of excellence that defines my five elements of excellence

- Children build emotional walls to protect themselves from bad relationships with family members

- If you want to make a difference in your family, you must break down the walls and create a safe place for communication

Chapter 5
Learning How to Tap In

To tell you the truth, it wasn't until more money came into the equation that I reconsidered how I was allocating my time and energy. If I had to give anybody advice about chasing their passion while keeping their family together, I'd tell them to look at home first. Look at your children. Look at your wife, husband, or partner and try to come up with an idea. Time is everything, and utilizing that time will allow you to get to know your family on a more personal level.

Remember when I mentioned earlier how I had a coach that pushed me towards my gift? Well, he also showed me how to tap in at an early age. Some of it was emotional. I recall an incident in which he challenged me.

He asked, "What's the worst thing that's ever happened to you?"

I replied, "Being a kid with no parents."

Coach then said, "Every time you run, I want you to think about the finish line and think that *that's* the man that gave your mama some heroin." I know it was harsh. I cried when he said that, but I used it and unleashed the beast. Once he captured my attention, Coach learned my story by asking me questions. Then he used elements of my past (at the time, my reality) as fuel.

The Art of Tapping In

Parents and mentors, this section is really special. This is a place for children to open up and talk because learning to "tap in" is about them. In this section, you're challenged to simply listen to your children. Put yourself in their shoes, and listen to what they say with three things in mind:

- Building Trust

- Space

- Respect

Building Trust

Earlier, I discussed the relationship I had with my guardians. Because of the way they treated me, I had a low level of trust in them. That lack of trust led to me not sharing different life experiences with them. I missed out on the opportunity to bounce things off of a parent.

As parents and advisors, we must recognize that life is about experiences. You must be open to talking to children about the broad range of things that happen to them and give them a safe-sounding board. These things include hard topics such as sex, bullying, and relationships.

You want to be the person your child comes to when they make decisions, not the person they avoid. Even when children do something wrong, you still need to let them know that they can talk to you. In fact, it's especially important that we talk about the mistakes with respect and trust.

Space

Some parents feel the need to be "helicopter parents." This means they hover over their child's every move. I believe that if a child is given space, they have the freedom to learn on their own how to become independent. Our ultimate goal as parents is to teach our children to become independent adults. Space is necessary to develop independence. Remember two things:

1. *Do not overcrowd children to the point where they feel bombarded.* A tale-tell sign you're overcrowding your child is when you become overly absorbed with helping your child make decisions.

Though we want to see them achieve more and be their best, we are over nurturing and don't give them room to think. I want my son to go to college and be on a track team. If I put my desires on him, I'm not giving him room to decide for himself. I'm making decisions for him. I'm overcrowding him. Don't do that. Instead, allow your children to grow on their own.

2. *Do not micromanage!* Micromanaging is something we also do to our kids. This involves giving them a task and not allowing them to complete what we asked. In fact, we begin to take on the task ourselves and not give them a chance to work. Before they can do the work or make a mistake, we step in and take over.

You must give them the space they need to learn how to complete tasks because this type of work helps them with their decision-making skills.

Give children the room to make better choices because this leads to growth. If you see them make a bad choice, step back and give them room to think it through. Recognizing these mistakes will help the child learn so they can make better choices in the future.

Space is not about giving children room. Space is about giving them better guidance and taking a different approach to making better decisions.

Respect by Responding, not Reacting

I'd like to share a personal story to demonstrate what I mean by reaction versus response:

One day, I turned the corner of our stairwell to hear my boys shouting at each other.

"Get out of my room!"

"I'm sick of you guys, and I can't take it anymore."

I rushed to the room to see what was happening. My oldest son was in a standoff with his two younger brothers. I have never seen him look so serious.

I said, "Son, what is going on here? You need to stop screaming at your brothers and calm down."

He replied, "See, Dad, you always take their side, but this is my room, and I want them out!"

I stopped for a moment and got really quiet. I reached out my hand to my son and said, "Son, I get it; they're in your space. We will leave your room, but I need you to take a deep breath. Everything is going to be alright."

It was amazing. As I sat and gave my oldest son my full attention, his voice lowered from an angry tone. He began to calm down. Then he said, "Dad, I know I was loud, I'm sorry." He continued to share more about his day and other feelings. I simply listened.

There are a couple of things I realized in that moment.

First, my son needed his space. Not only that, but he needed my compassion, not my reaction. I learned that day how to respond versus how to react. Reacting would have been yelling at my son or punishing him for yelling at his brothers. Instead, I chose to respond by hearing what he was saying and understanding what he needed in that moment.

There are two things I believe we should remember when working with kids:

1. Never yell or "trip out."

2. Stay in control, and show compassion.

Exercise 5.1: Building Trust

List things that you believe are hurtful about your current relationship with your child and allow your child to do the same.

_____

_____

_____

_____

_____

_____

_____

_____

_____

_____

_____

_____

_____

_____

_____

_____

_____

_____

Parent, Mentor, Guardian List:

_____

_____

_____

_____

_____

_____

_____

_____

_____

_____

_____

_____

_____

_____

_____

_____

_____

_____

_____

_____

_____

_____

_____

_____

_____

_____

_____

_____

_____

_____

Child List:

_____

_____

_____

_____

_____

_____

_____

_____

_____

_____

_____

_____

_____

_____

_____

_____

_____

_____

_____

_____

_____

_____

_____

_____

_____

_____

_____

Now that you both have identified things you feel are harmful to your relationship use the statement below to begin a conversation about ONE thing on each list.

"I want to talk to you about _____ and how it can affect the rest of your life. I love you, and I feel like talking about this will help both of us."

Reiterate your love for them.

Here are some ways to guide the conversation with your child:

- Allow them to pick from their list *and* your list. This gives them a chance to address issues on both lists

- Discuss everything on each list.

- If your discussion begins to break down, stop and decide a different time to finish talking after calming down.

EXPECTED RESULTS

- To be the person your child will go to when they make decisions, not the one they avoid.

- Help your child analyze how to talk about their mistakes

- Help your child make better decisions

SUMMARY — LEARNING HOW TO TAP IN

- Build trust

- Give children personal space

- Respect children's boundaries

- Respond; don't react

Chapter 6
Rethink, Revitalize, Rebuild

Dumb Things We Do that Hurt Our Kids

This is a very important chapter because it will help you establish something extremely important. It focuses on SELF EXPECTATIONS. The best way for me to explain this is to paint a simple picture.

I grew up around a lot of "C" students. This is not a bad thing, but the standard for success was set at just passing. If you could pass, then you would finish. The problem is that just passing is basic. When you *aim* low, you *land* low. I believe parents and children have to look beyond their circumstances. They have to set goals and expectations that require stretching. When you stretch, one of two things will happen: growth or circulation.

When you grow, you expand your mind to see new things. This helps you envision your future in different places and have the confidence to strive for something greater. Circulation occurs when you begin to see things differently and feel more confident. Over time, confidence will help you find the courage you need to explore new things. While growth is about allowing yourself to be open to new things, circulation is about exploring those new things once they are identified. So setting higher expectations will ultimately lead you to growth and circulation.

" Give Your Child a Chance to Be an Individual" -RD

Showing Love

A child needs to feel loved by their parent. The child that doesn't feel loved seeks love in other places. This can lead to gang interest, promiscuous sex, drugs, or hanging with the wrong crowd. If you don't show children love, the streets will gladly take your place.

Every child is internally screaming, "CAN YOU LOVE ME?

- How do you show love?
- Talk to them
- Hug them
- Show them how to do something they're interested in doing
- Watch a movie and be present
- Spend time with your child

Showing love is one of many ways that you can nurture your relationship. You should treat it a lot like you would a new plant. Essentially, you must water the relationship, so it can grow. This means spending time with them so they will feel like you care and that you will listen to them.

Think about the future and your relationship with your child. Ask yourself, "What kind of relationship do I *really* want to have with my child?" Whatever image comes to your mind, you must work on it daily. Every moment you spend with your child is building up to the future relationship you see in your mind.

It's not about money or what you can buy; it's about the time spent together. Make sure you plan to spend time with them and show them that every moment is important.

Stop Trying to Live Through Them

I recently mentored a young actress who began rebelling against her mother. She broke down emotionally and even ran away from home. As a child, she was excellent at acting, but having her mom involved in her career was too much. Before filming, they would argue all the way to and from the set.

The mom was very passionate about her child, but for the wrong reasons. The mother began living through the child. She put pressure on her daughter to perform well. The daughter felt as if her ability to act was the only reason her mother loved her. Of course, we *know* this isn't true, but this is what happens when parents begin living out their dreams through their children. Sports, music, and academics are all activities that parents can unintentionally over-manage with a child.

How do you keep yourself from becoming this type of parent?

Think about this:

- Just because your child has similar qualities to you, it doesn't mean they are your clone

- Don't confuse wanting the best for your child with living through them.

- Listen to your child

- Understand your child's passion

- Be supportive, not directive

You don't have to be your child's manager. In many cases, the best person to help your child perform at optimum levels is a coach or other person outside the family. This type of relationship eliminates bias, reduces uncomfortable conversations, and takes away the pressure on the family. Certain celebrities have family members as partners and have lost their families due to bad breakups.

When it's time to make big life decisions, you want to be in a supportive role, not an authoritative role. There is a point when your child needs to think as an individual, and your relationship will be important. Remember, you always want to be the parent they come to when they make decisions, not the parent they avoid.

Positive Feedback Over Verbal Abuse

There is a big difference between giving positive feedback and being verbally abusive. Often parents confuse the two because they have an emotional attachment to their kid. When the child makes a mistake, the parent wants to find a way to discuss how to make better decisions.

Verbal abuse begins when a parent repeats over, and over the one thing a child has done wrong. Every day is a fresh start. Has your child ever screamed, "Don't throw my mistakes in my face?" Well, this is an example of verbal abuse. Every time you repeat their mistakes to them, you take them backward. As parents, we want children to remember the mistake, thinking this will keep them from repeating it.

"Your last report was terrible, and this is why you make bad grades."

"You stole money out of my purse and got caught; now I can never trust you."

"You snuck out of the house and got caught, and now I can't trust you to be home."

"You got kicked out of school, and I can't trust you to make good decisions."

Our job as parents is to stimulate our child's mind about how to do things better and think through tough situations. When we confuse verbal abuse with positive feedback, we disconnect ourselves from the child. The child feels like you will regurgitate the same embarrassing words again. They get frustrated and begin acting out or protecting themselves from you.

Here is what I learned from my own experience with verbal abuse as a child:

- It made me feel "less than."
- I had anxiety.
- I felt suicidal because I was a screw-up.
- I felt like I couldn't compete in this world.

The words made me feel worse every time I heard

them. Sometimes, I felt even worse than when *I* made the mistake! Moral of the story is simple: be positive, not belittling. Even though they're kids, they can be easily offended too.

Learning Responsibility vs. Being an Adult Child

We often don't give kids a chance to be kids. In an effort to teach them responsibility, we sometimes give too many adult-like responsibilities to our children.

> *"Give your child household responsibilities, but it's not fair to expect them to run your house. They need their child moments." -RD*

I want my 10-year-old to enjoy being ten. I want him to play and have fun. There is a time to be moms and dads, a role that is an irreversible adult role. There are financial and emotional situations that can lead a family to depend on their children to run a household in the absence of a parent; as much as I understand that-be careful! These roles can cause a child to miss childhood. They also push a child to make adult-like decisions before they are responsible enough to handle them.

This situation makes children resent not being able to be a kid. Give your children a chance to be young. When it is time to be an adult, they can't go back to being a kid.

Stopping Generational Behavior

The way you were raised can have a huge impact on how you respond to your child when you're not getting what you want from them. Some parents find themselves uttering negative words or swearing at their children to get them to do what they want. This points back to generational behavior. If your parents treated you a certain way or responded in a certain way, you may carry that behavior into your life. This means treating your children in the same way you were treated, which is *exactly* what we're trying to avoid.

I believe name-calling and cursing at your children breaks their character, makes them have low self-esteem, and makes them feel like no one cares. In many cases, children look up to their parents. When you break them in this way, it really has an impact on the way they feel about themselves. It also affects the way they feel about you. As parents and even as mentors, we should really rethink the way we talk to our children. Words are like swords when used the wrong way:

they can cut deep, emotional wounds that are hard to heal.

As a parent and a person, you must find your own path to success with your children. This means separating from your past and doing what is best for your family today. In communication, this means rethinking the behaviors of your parents and stepping back to look at what hurt you most about the way they responded and talked to you. Let's take a moment to work through this for a better understanding.

Exercise: Identifying the Hurt

Write down the most hurtful things you heard from your family growing up.

_____

_____

_____

_____

_____

_____

_____

_____

_____

_____

_____

_____

_____

_____

_____

_____

_____

_____

_____

_____

_____

Now share in a few words how those statements made you feel?

_____

_____

_____

_____

_____

_____

_____

_____

_____

_____

_____

_____

_____

_____

_____

_____

_____

_____

_____

_____

_____

_____

_____

_____

_____

Now take a moment and think about a few names you have called your child that hurt them.

_____

_____

_____

_____

_____

_____

_____

_____

_____

_____

_____

_____

_____

_____

_____

_____

_____

_____

_____

_____

_____

_____

How do you think hearing you call them that made them feel?

_____

_____

_____

_____

_____

_____

_____

_____

_____

_____

_____

_____

_____

_____

_____

_____

_____

_____

_____

_____

_____

SUMMARY: RETHINK, REVITALIZE, & REBUILD

- Setting goals will help your kids' either grow or circulate

- Showing love ensures that you're nurturing the relationship with your children

- Trying to live your dreams through your kids can cause long-term trauma and resentment

- Opt for positive feedback over verbal abuse to keep the lines of communication open between you and your child

- Breaking generational curses involves creating your own path in parenthood

Chapter 7
Skills To Be Successful

There are several skills that we want to instill in our children to make sure they are successful. The ones highlighted here are the most basic and will put them on the right track to gathering other important life skills as well.

Setting Goals

Earlier in the book, I mentioned goals related to accomplishment. Now there are some specific goal-related things I believe EVERY child should learn. In my approach to teaching about these things, I have developed a set of ways to learn how to set goals.

The Report Card Method

In our house, we use report cards as a measure of performance on goals. Our kids set academic goals, and they are responsible for meeting them. By learning this disciplined approach early, they are much more likely to become very successful adults.

Financial Literacy

Financial literacy is something that needs to be incorporated into a child's life at an early age

It must be clear to your child that they have financial responsibility. This means that they must learn to earn money and then be disciplined with it. Earning money is where everything in financial literacy starts. It is the basis for the decisions we all make about our money.

Question: *How* do children earn money? Whether it's through chores or a part-time job, it must be clear that to earn money, you must work. Work can be cleaning the house or cutting the neighbor's yard. It is anything children do that provides money in exchange for their services/work. After they have made money, then the decisions about how it is used can begin. This is where discipline comes in, and this is where most parents fail to discuss some really important topics with their kids, such as:

- Saving
- Paying bills
- Having a budget
- Building credit

Growing up, I was not taught how to manage money. I was also not taught how to seek out work. Seeking work is mowing lawns, taking the neighbor's trash out; anything you can do to earn money. Now that I'm older, I recognize that if these skills had been introduced to me at an early age, my life would be different. It's important for me to teach my children how to budget, save, and invest.

In our community, it's common that many parents don't understand the importance of sharing this knowledge with their kids. I believe that investing quality time with them and sharing more about money will change the way future generations handle money and life.

Discipline (Parent and the Child)

Our kids should be learning about discipline because it both shapes behavior and teaches them important ideals about the way they should think. Discipline is about making the decision to do things a certain way and being willing to work hard.

I have developed something called the Four Principles of Discipline, which I have incorporated into my family life. If implemented correctly, these principles will help you be more efficient in every area of your life, whether at work, in school, and even during extracurricular activities.

The Four Principles of Discipline include:

- Working Hard

- Being Obedient

- Limiting Yourself

- Showing Up

Don Norford, my track coach at Long Beach Polytech, provides a great example of how each of these principles can be put into action as it relates to your children. He was a tough coach who hand-picked me to attend this special school. Don saw my talent in track and pulled me aside. He explained how he thought I had a gift and helped me get into the school. He introduced me to his system, and it was a system that trained a lot of successful athletes to perform at their best.

He instilled in me a food, training, and performance regimen I will never forget. After a pep talk, I won multiple races as I envisioned my mom waiting for me at the finish line. It was my first experience with having a vision and setting a goal. I actually ended up having a couple of them.

My first goal was to win as often as possible. What would it take for me to win like this? I had to have a plan and follow it to the letter. Ultimately, I had to be disciplined. Don helped me with my plan by instilling certain qualities in me as an athlete.

My second goal was to be one of the best track runners in the school's history. I also had a huge desire to win that came from having Don as a mentor; I wanted to make him proud. All of this led me to a state championship, and I got there using my four principles of discipline. Take a look at what that process looked like below:

Work Hard. Hard work meant I had to train harder than I had ever trained for anything in my life. In my neighborhood, it seemed like everyone was a fast runner. I had to be better than everyone I knew and some people I didn't know. Because of the amount of competition, I had to change.

Obedience. I couldn't be inconsistent; I had to stick to my plan. I had to practice as often as possible and be very focused.

Limit Yourself. This meant being different from other teen boys and not chasing all the girls. I had to take control of that area of my life and not do what everyone else was doing.

Show Up. Last, I had to show up for track and be ready to perform. Up until that point, I had never had enough structure in my life to consistently show up anywhere. Showing up means being there, being ready, and taking the time to show how much you want something. It was crazy, but I realized that my showing up was making me better.

On June 15, 1995, all my work paid off. On that day, I won a state championship and changed my life forever.

Time Management

Time management is a key value in life. If you can't manage your time, you can't be successful.

Time management for children can include:

- Getting up and dressed for school
- Getting assignments done and turned in on time

You have to take managing your time seriously because your entire plan can fall apart if you don't manage your time well. I didn't realize how important time management was until I became an adult.

My first boss said to me, "You have to be on time!" I got a great job that was a privilege and an opportunity. And then I lost that job because I was casual about my time. I didn't hear the warning that being on time was important.

Time is about commitment and discipline. When you have a commitment to show up, someone else is depending on your honor and your word. You must be disciplined enough to keep your word. If you don't grasp this concept early, you will miss out on so many opportunities. Additionally, you can get a bad reputation. Time management is a key value in life. If you can't manage your time, you can't be successful.

How Can You Help Your Child Be Successful with Time Management?

The greatest influence on me for time management was my family. They didn't take time management seriously. They were late to everything, and at times didn't show up at all! I believe you have to make it clear to your children that time management is important, and you also have to put the responsibility for it in their hands. The way you do this is by giving them something specific to do with a deadline. This creates a better understanding of time management by giving them ownership.

On the other hand, there are also consequences to missing a deadline. For my sons, missing a deadline is a quick way to lose their video game privileges. This is definitely what you want your child to understand. It's not just about being on time; it's about managing the process of time. Planning, preparing, and executing on time are all extremely important.

Exposure to Something Better

We have to find a way to expose our kids to something different. The skills listed above aren't enough. If we want more for our children, then we have to *give* them more. When you take the initiative to show children something more than just "what is expected," you build relationships they will remember. Most importantly, their skillset will be sharpened and their future a little brighter.

Here are a few suggestions on how to expose your kids to something better:

1. Hone their craft by finding programs and events that show them the possibilities
2. Get in the car and take them to places that are different from your neighborhood
3. Watch YouTube and TV shows with them about topics that pique their interest
4. Show them pictures of people, places, and things you feel could make them better

In chapter one, you did a gift inventory and discussed it with your child. This is a moment when you can help your child experience and use their gift.

On-Campus Programs

A friend of mine has a daughter who is considered "gifted and talented." She learned to read at age three, and this has opened many doors for her and her parents. One door, in particular, is a math and science program for girls held on a university campus. The father signed up his daughter, expecting a few weekend science lessons.

Instead, it opened up a whole new world for the father and the daughter. She learned to apply math and science to life. Even more importantly, she was spending time on a campus with college students. One particular young lady became a mentor and helped his daughter set some goals. Now she is like a Big Sister who checks on his daughter regularly. His daughter said to him after the first event, "Daddy, I want to go to this college one day." He had never talked to her about college because she was only eight. But that one decision—to sign her up for the program—began changing their life.

Go to College. Leave Home. Leave the Cocoon.

I encourage all students to leave home. It helps them become independent and learn how to live in the world. I suggest college, trade school, or even a few semesters at a junior college. This is a way to grow into their independence. It is a chance to think outside the confines of their parent's home and become an adult in their own right.

Exercise: Identifying a Skillset

Now that you understand the importance of skills, it's time to think critically about the skills that your child possesses. List seven skills you think you child should have to be successful.

Skill #1

Skill #2

Skill #3

Skill #4

Skill #5

Skill #6

Skill #7

Now that you have listed these skills, use the space below to reflect on why you think these skills are needed for your child to be successful.

_____

_____

_____

_____

_____

_____

_____

_____

_____

_____

_____

_____

_____

_____

_____

_____

_____

_____

_____

_____

_____

_____

_____

SUMMARY: SKILLS TO SUCCESS

- Setting goals adds structure to your child's life and gives them something toward which they can work.

- The four principles of discipline are designed to help you and your children be more efficient in every area of your life.

- Exposing your kids to more opportunities will help them achieve success faster.

Chapter 8

I'm Trying to Help You Change Your Life

I'm not your enemy, I'm your coach. --RD

Your kids haven't really started living their lives yet. You hope they understand that you're trying to help them on their journey to a great life. Often, kids don't comprehend who their parents are or what their job as a parents is. Parents' God-given job is to guide their children, protect them, and show them the way. They must act as a force field where no weapon can harm them and watch out for mistakes that work as detours as children navigate their road to success. This is the same for mentors, counselors, and anyone working with children.

Kids don't see that; they often see their parents as the enemy. Practice how to say these words to your children: I'm not here to be your enemy. I'm not here to be your enemy. I'm here because I was placed in your life to be your help to a better life.

Parents must consistently and regularly communicate to the children that you are their guardian and protector. As their parents, you are their role models. Provide little reminders to your child, letting them know that you're not their enemy, but their help—the kind of help that can guide them to great success. These reminders can take the form of encouraging handwritten notes in their book bags or lunch boxes and showing up to parent/teacher night as advocates for your children. Be opportunistic when delivering these little reminders.

As parents, our role is to help our children create a plan, not control their lives. Parents want to help their kids navigate through obstacles so they can be successful. People think that a parent showing their worry or showing that they care is a screen for controlling the child. It's not. It's truly just showing the love needed to help our children grow into their independence.

Parents are coaches to children. We guide them to make good decisions in life like coaches guide athletes to make great plays in a game.

An Example of the Parent's Role

I have a friend who has reached the point in life where her daughter is 18 years old and wants to date older men. My friend sees that the men her daughter is bringing around are not responsible. Experience has taught the mom how to spot a good man. In fact, she sees a particular man the daughter is dating as the type of man that would make her daughter "the other woman." She has expressed her concern, but the daughter only sees her mom as a controlling parent. This has created a struggle between them. Let's take a deeper look.

The Mom's Side

The mom wants the daughter to breathe and understand the mom's position without feeling threatened. There are feelings, emotions, and attitudes to overcome. The child's response has not been positive. What does a parent do in a situation like this?

Steps to approaching hard topics:

1. Be subtle with your approach, not aggressive.
2. Talk to the child and understand where their mind is on this subject, so you can respond without showing bias.
3. Show the child the BIG picture from a wider lens; try to get the child to look outside themselves, take themselves out of the situation, or put someone else in their shoes.
4. No matter if the child does or doesn't follow your advice—**you must still love them**. Allow children to make mistakes so that they can experience the growth that comes from lessons

learned. My grandmother (my trusted guardian) often told me not to do certain things and later had the post-conversation. I would always come back and say, "Grandmother, I should have listened to you."

The Child's Side

The child should always remember that the parent's role is to be a guardian (guardian=a defender, protector, or keeper). Children should use their parents as role models. Good or bad, children will learn from their parents how to make better decisions.

Nine times out of ten, children will find that parents are wise counsel. They're there to give instructions and valid advice to best suit the child's life. Children must realize that the parent is not there to hurt them but instead to help them. If children are coachable, it will help them grow. Again, you must share this perspective with your children so that they can make better decisions.

IMPORTANT POINT: Not all kids are fortunate to have parents they can look up to in this way. In this instance, the child should look to mentors for wise counsel. The best way to judge whether a mentor is truly wise counsel is to pay attention to their lives. Are they making good decisions? If they are, then follow their advice on big decisions. Making decisions alone can be dangerous.

What is Important?

The most important point is the relationship between a parent and a child. For this to remain strong, we must reduce barriers to communication and the number of conflicts. Looking at both sides of the discussion helps everyone know their role. Again, parents are in place to help their children create a plan and live better lives.

Exercise Questions

Have you experienced this type of behavior from your child? (Yes/No)

What did you do to help them?

_____

_____

_____

_____

_____

_____

_____

_____

_____

_____

_____

_____

_____

_____

_____

_____

_____

_____

_____

_____

_____

What role did you play in the discussion?

- Were you the listener?
- Were you aggressive?
- Were you the accuser?

What was your approach

- Did you scream at them?
- Did you freeze because you were in shock?

If so, refer back to those four important skills mention earlier; you should be looking at the situation like this:

Did you listen, and were you a good listener?

Did you refrain from reacting until they told you everything?

Did you put yourself in their shoes? Not judgmental and opinionated?

Did you break away from parent mode and just listen to them?

This exercise should help you begin to frame conversations with your children when faced with challenging situations. Use the space below to takes notes:

_____

_____

_____

_____

_____

_____

_____

_____

_____

_____

_____

_____

_____

_____

_____

_____

_____

_____

_____

_____

_____

_____

SUMMARY: TRYING TO CHANGE YOUR LIFE

- Your role is to help your child create a plan, not control their lives.

- Never be aggressive when talking through difficult topics.

- Your kids should be comfortable coming to you for advice.

Chapter 9
Goals

Although we touched on this briefly in another chapter, I want to take a moment to highlight just how important it is to set goals and have your children do the same. Setting goals gives us purpose. Whether we are a parent, mentor, or child, having a goal gives us something to work towards and provides us with a focus. If we didn't set goals, then we would easily get distracted or sidetracked by things that aren't important. Have a higher expectation of yourself. Plan and set short-term and long-term goals that will help with your success. If you set the bar high and reach for it, then you will push yourself to higher levels of success.

Setting goals is really important for your child's success. Let me be clear: setting goals is challenging. It requires focus and execution—two things that even adults struggle with regularly. Because setting goals lead you to success, you want to ensure your own goal-setting techniques are succinct. After all, you're the one who will be teaching these same techniques to your kids.

Types of Goals

Goals can be short-term or long-term. You should understand the difference and help your children to set both types.

Short-term goals are realistic goals that you can control. Examples for your child include:

- Make sure my grades stay up.

- Set a schedule and follow it.

I like to set weekly goals because it gives me a reason to challenge myself often. Goal setting can be as small as saving $50 to buy some tennis shoes. It's something you feel really confident you can accomplish in a short period of time.

Long term goals are more focused on the future. These are harder to determine because it requires the passing of time. Unfortunately, time can affect goals because life situations impact your time. Job loss, death, or family transitions can all affect long-term goals. I believe the key to achieving long-term goals is to follow your weekly goals. Here are a few examples of long-term goals:

- Buy a home

- Graduate from school

- Get a job

- Start a career

Here is my "secret sauce" for accomplishing goals (short- and long-term):

- Determination

- Consistency

- Dedication

- Hard work

One of my long-term goals is to begin buying property for each of my sons. I don't want them to pay mortgages or rent while they are in college. If they manage the properties well, they may never pay a mortgage or rent in life. This long-term goal will change the trajectory of my family forever. To make this goal happen, my wife and I had to change the way we live day-to-day.

Exercise: Short- and Long-Term Goals (Parent and Student Exercise)

Both parent and student should individually do this exercise, then come together and discuss what they have written. Also, the parent and student should discuss their roles in helping each other accomplish their goals.

Write down five short-term goals you want to accomplish this year.

1.

2.

3.

4.

5.

Now write down five long-term goals you want to accomplish in the next five years.

1.

2.

3.

4.

5.

Now look at the short-term goals and decide what resources are needed to accomplish each goal.

Goal 1:

Resources needed:

Goal 2:

Resources needed:

Goal 3:

Resources needed:

Goal 4:

Resources needed:

Goal 5:

Resources needed:

Now sit together with your child and discuss each other's roles in helping accomplish the goals both you and your child have set.

SUMMARY: GOALS

- Setting goals gives you and your child purpose.

- Short-term goals are realistic objectives you can accomplish in under three months.

- Long-term goals are objectives that focus on the future.

- Accomplishing goals requires determination, consistency, dedication, and hard work.

Chapter 10
Building Character in Your Child

There are five important factors in building character in your children. I believe the following five things are the most critical:

- *Integrity.* Doing what is right when no one is looking.

- *Listening Skills.* Stop, hear, and process.

- *Being Coachable.* Be willing to take critiques and correction, and use the information to im prove yourself.

- *Having a Mentor.* Find a role model that has experience, has endured, has sustained, and is successful in what they do.

- *Setting Goals.* Have higher expectations for yourself. Plan to set short-term and long-term goals that will help with your success. If you set the bar high and reach for it, then you will push yourself to higher levels of success.

Integrity

Life events can challenge a child to think for themselves. If they are not prepared, they may make decisions that can cost them a lifetime. Integrity is a root, a base, an anchor in which to make all decisions. If you instill the importance of integrity in your children, then you will not have to worry about their decisions because you will know the basis of how they think. Here is an example of where I had to teach one of my sons the importance of integrity.

My Son's Journey

My son once reached a point in life where fitting in was very important. Like most children, he made a decision to do something that compromised his integrity. What is done in the dark always comes to the light. If you are known as a thief, people won't trust you. I wondered how I could help him understand that this was a bad decision. I asked him how he should be punished. He gave me his ideas.

As a parent, this was important. It made it clear to me that he understood there were consequences for his actions.

As a parent, you must analyze and evaluate to understand what you're dealing with and to know if your children are in a position to change or turn around.

What level of discipline is necessary? Not all kids need a harsh disciplinarian. The important thing is that you engage in conversation with them to grow their understanding of integrity. This is a way of providing guidance, building a relationship, and leading them to be able to make better decisions on their own.

Be A Good Listener

Stop, hear, and process are the three habits you should encourage your child to develop so that they can become a good listener. What kids need to understand is that we are trying to help them. Listening to you, the parent, and not responding like we are out to get them is a vital trait. Not assuming we are ready to punish them without hearing the story.

Encouraging Them To Stop

Children have their own mindset. We have to remember that we can't be everywhere, so it is important to show them what we mean when we say STOP. In this case, we are asking them to never make a decision too fast. Never assume things before the evidence is available. Most important, wait long enough to be sure whatever situation you're in, you understand the facts. Also, they must take the time to explain everything so that no one is left to assume unanswered questions.

Encouraging Them To Hear

Sometimes kids have earplugs in, and they want to do their own thing. Listening can save their lives. If I tell my son, "In the state of California, you can't walk outside wearing a red rag," it can save his life. This color is a well-known gang color, and knowing this can save their life. If they act like they have earplugs and don't listen, it can be dangerous. You must help your child understand the importance of listening to you and other adults. Our guidance is based on life lessons. We just have to share them with our kids and encourage them to open their ears... Take off the earplugs.

Be Coachable

Like I mentioned earlier, you can't help someone who doesn't want the help. It's important that children are susceptible to your teachings and not too closed off.

Having A Mentor

Mentors are important because they provide children

with direction. There is someone that wants to coach them to be successful. Mentors have a lot to do with your children's success because they spend quality time with your children, helping them in ways you may not be able to.

Mentors hold children accountable for what they say. A good mentor will remind you when you "say one thing but do something different." Mentors can be selected based on careers, community leadership, family friendships, or something else. What is significant is that they align with something your child can set goals around and grow.

Setting Goals

Setting goals is crucial for your child's success. We dedicated a whole chapter to this, but just understand that it's integral to character-building.

SUMMARY: BUILD CHARACTER

- Building character involves integrity, listening skills, being coachable, having a mentor, and setting goals.

- Encourage your child to never make rash decisions without thinking things through.

Chapter 11

Every Child's Life Matters

Do you remember the third grade? I remember that year of my life vividly. It was a disaster in my mind for a long time. Now, I am able to see it as my first test, a test that defines my way of handling life situations.

My teacher was Ms. Kessleman, and she kept me close to her. When I say close, I mean really close. My desk was right next to hers. She watched my every move and pushed me to do my work. The problem was I had trouble doing my work. So I began acting out in class. I was the funny man, or so I thought. I was also the person that couldn't read well.

Many days, Ms. Kessleman would ask me to read. It was like scratching your fingers on a chalkboard. I struggled to get through every word. My classmates would laugh at me. I felt horrible, but I didn't know how to fix my problem. I became more frustrated and even angry. I felt like she was giving me too much attention, and in response, I acted out.

One day she sent me to meet Mr. Leroy and he asked me a lot of questions. I thought she was sending me to meet someone who was going to help me. Instead, it turned out quite different. You see, Mr. Leroy was assessing my ability, and he sent a message to Ms. Kessleman I will never forget. "Ms. Kessleman, based on our findings, Robert is a slow learner and needs to be enrolled in special education classes."

Wait—what? I thought I was doing great. Ms. Kessleman was my BFF, and everything was fine. I felt so betrayed and hurt. Was she saying I was slow? Was she about to put me in a class of misfits? How did I survive? How would I overcome that first shocking moment?

My living situation was unstable because I had to go to a special school. My new teacher did everything she could to comfort me, but I withdrew. This is when I started developing my walls. I couldn't trust anyone. I was being abused at home, I had a learning disability, and I felt so insecure. I truly think my life would not be where it is today if I had not experienced what happened after that day. This is the root of how I got the idea to write and create this workbook.

There I was, staring out a window in West LA. Nothing about my life was a storybook. I lived with my grandmother because my parents were gone. Heroine, or "Heron," as they used to call it, left me alone. My grandmother refused to let me go into the system, so she pulled me into a complex life. We lived in a house with seven people, including my abusive uncle. What did that mean for me? Security, a roof over my head, a place to call home?

Yes and no.

I survived that complex life—a chapter filled with drama, abuse, and things that would make you believe failure was imminent. But not only did I survive, but I'm also now walking into my stride. I have four sons and a lovely wife. We have a beautiful home, and we are moving forward.

I believe there are some key things that helped me overcome something many people would have failed. I want to help more people survive. I want to show you some survival skills to make your relationship with your kids a lasting, loving piece of your life.

My life is about breaking the chains of a prior generation—our habits, our behaviors, and the crazy way we raise our kids. I always say, "You do what you learn, even if what you have learned is wrong."

I started this chapter off with my story to say this: every child deserves a shot at happiness. Every child deserves for their voice to be heard and their needs to be met. No matter what they're going through, their life matters. As parents and as mentors, we are obligated to ensure we do everything possible to make them realize just how important their life is and, most importantly, what it could be.

Four Pillars That Changed My Life

I had four people who I believe helped me make a major decision in my life. That decision was to break the chains that linked me to family behaviors of destruction. I call these people my four pillars. They are my Grandmother, Aunt Mary, Aunt BJ, and my Uncle.

Let me explain who they were and why they matter. Take a look at the next page.

	Grandma	Aunt Mary	Aunt BJ	Uncle
About Them	• She was the Influence I needed • She believed in what was right and she shared her values with other people • She was my hero	• Her mission was to make sure I understood the streets • She taught me to hustle and not to trust	• She was always the life of the party • Loved to entertain • Never scared to share her gifts	• He thought that insulting and making me feel horrible would make me a better person • Got in trouble with no explanation as to why
How I Was Impacted?	• She taught me to be an influencer, work hard and want more out of life • Showed me how to love a family, lead them and be strong • Because of her I strive to be successful and a good person	• She showed me not to let your habits impair your ability to reason and think • She taught me to love unconditionally	• I am super outgoing because of her • I am the life of the party • I always show up when I am put on the spot	• His actions taught me what not to do with my children • Because of him I always listen to what is going on and not act of frustration

Recognizing the influencers in your life helps you to look at the big picture of why you are the way you are and what you learned from them is so important. As parents and mentors, we want to be on our children's lists of "pillars" who influence them. We want to be the positive influence in their lives and truly be who they need us to be. Before that can happen, we must evaluate our own lives first.

Exercise: Who Are Your Influencers?

Let's take a look at your life and talk about *your* key influencers.

Who influenced the way you handle life situations?

Name				
About Them				
How I Was Impacted?				

Creating A Roadmap

I want you to walk away with something powerful. I want you to have a roadmap. I want you to understand your child better.

I want to help you turn your child's weaknesses into strengths.

Are you ready for the next step?

BREAKING THE CHAINS CHALLENGE

In spite of my environment, I broke the chains. I was born to a heroin-addicted mother. My father was murdered just months before I came into this world. I lived in an environment that was encouraging but also thrived on fear, bullying, and abuse. The good news is, I broke the chains.

Now I have a family, and my wife Christi and I are raising four awesome boys, and I have to admit, we have an incredibly blessed life. I'm issuing a challenge based on all the things I believe it took to get out of my situation and break the chains.

In 2019, I saw how being challenged to do something BIG with your life can help you. With this book, I'm issuing a challenge to my community. I want to work with you to help you improve your relationship with your children. In each chapter, I broke down the individual pieces of a system. A system that I believe can change lives. I want to start with you, and help more people like us--one person, one family at a time. It's time to take the challenge and break the chains.

A SPECIAL THANK YOU

I thank my wife Christi Daniels and children RJ, Dylan, Tristan and Houston who have honestly been my backbone. They are the reason this book was even possible. I thank God for you all.

To my forever queen, which is my grandmother, for having such high expectations for me and always believing in me no matter what. I love how you taught me to push myself despite struggles and to make sure to put God first no matter what. RIH Mommy, I will always live by your motto "Love is the Answer".

To my Aunt BJ who raised me like her son, I always looked up to you and admired your strength, spirt and determination. RIH.

To my Brother, Aunts, Uncles and Cousins, you all had a part in raising me and are part of the reason I am who I am today. I thank you and appreciate you.

To my Mother-in-law and sisters-in-laws I thank you for always supporting me and having my back no matter what. The love you exude makes this world a better place.

To my cousin Will and good friend Terelle, thank you for your contributions and all of your great advise and feedback about the book

To every friend, family member, church member, business partner, co-worker or associate I thank you for being a part of my life.

I thank God for this opportunity to be an uncompromising force for good and to do my part in making this world a better place.

Made in the USA
Columbia, SC
25 September 2022

67757025R00086